# PET LOVER'S PASSWORD KEEPER

## A Fun Way to Organize Your Online Accounts

*(Large Print 8.5 x 11 Paperback Edition)*

*From the Paw Prints Collection™*
*Large Print Password Organizer for Pet Lovers*

*by*
Cynthia Owen

PET LOVER'S PASSWORD KEEPER

A Fun Way to Organize Your Online Accounts (Large Print 8.5 x 11 Paperback Edition)

From the Paw Prints Collection™



ISBN: 9781960577849

Published by JC Owen and Associates, Inc.

www.jcowensales.com

Printed in the United States of America

# This Notebook Belongs To:

_______________________

*"Paws and reflect on the good things in life."*

**Website / Account #**

**User Name / Email**

**Password / Hint**

**Notes**

**Website / Account #**

**User Name / Email**

**Password / Hint**

**Notes**

**Website / Account #**

**User Name / Email**

**Password / Hint**

**Notes**

A-B

**Website / Account #**

**User Name / Email**

**Password / Hint**

**Notes**

**Website / Account #**

**User Name / Email**

**Password / Hint**

**Notes**

**Website / Account #**

**User Name / Email**

**Password / Hint**

**Notes**

**Website / Account #**

**User Name / Email**

**Password / Hint**

**Notes**

**Website / Account #**

**User Name / Email**

**Password / Hint**

**Notes**

**Website / Account #**

**User Name / Email**

**Password / Hint**

**Notes**

**Website / Account #**

**User Name / Email**

**Password / Hint**

**Notes**

**Website / Account #**

**User Name / Email**

**Password / Hint**

**Notes**

**Website / Account #**

**User Name / Email**

**Password / Hint**

**Notes**

**Website / Account #**

**User Name / Email**

**Password / Hint**

**Notes**

**Website / Account #**

**User Name / Email**

**Password / Hint**

**Notes**

**Website / Account #**

**User Name / Email**

**Password / Hint**

**Notes**

**Website / Account #**

**User Name / Email**

**Password / Hint**

**Notes**

**Website / Account #**

**User Name / Email**

**Password / Hint**

**Notes**

**Website / Account #**

**User Name / Email**

**Password / Hint**

**Notes**

**Website / Account #**

**User Name / Email**

**Password / Hint**

**Notes**

**Website / Account #**

**User Name / Email**

**Password / Hint**

**Notes**

**Website / Account #**

**User Name / Email**

**Password / Hint**

**Notes**

**Website / Account #**

**User Name / Email**

**Password / Hint**

**Notes**

**Website / Account #**

**User Name / Email**

**Password / Hint**

**Notes**

**Website / Account #**

**User Name / Email**

**Password / Hint**

**Notes**

**Website / Account #**

**User Name / Email**

**Password / Hint**

**Notes**

**Website / Account #**

**User Name / Email**

**Password / Hint**

**Notes**

**Website / Account #**

**User Name / Email**

**Password / Hint**

**Notes**

C-D

**Website / Account #**

**User Name / Email**

**Password / Hint**

**Notes**

**Website / Account #**

**User Name / Email**

**Password / Hint**

**Notes**

**Website / Account #**

**User Name / Email**

**Password / Hint**

**Notes**

**Website / Account #**

**User Name / Email**

**Password / Hint**

**Notes**

**Website / Account #**

**User Name / Email**

**Password / Hint**

**Notes**

**Website / Account #**

**User Name / Email**

**Password / Hint**

**Notes**

**Website / Account #**

**User Name / Email**

**Password / Hint**

**Notes**

**Website / Account #**

**User Name / Email**

**Password / Hint**

**Notes**

**Website / Account #**

**User Name / Email**

**Password / Hint**

**Notes**

**Website / Account #**

**User Name / Email**

**Password / Hint**

**Notes**

**Website / Account #**

**User Name / Email**

**Password / Hint**

**Notes**

**Website / Account #**

**User Name / Email**

**Password / Hint**

**Notes**

**Website / Account #**

**User Name / Email**

**Password / Hint**

**Notes**

**Website / Account #**

**User Name / Email**

**Password / Hint**

**Notes**

**Website / Account #**

**User Name / Email**

**Password / Hint**

**Notes**

**Website / Account #**

**User Name / Email**

**Password / Hint**

**Notes**

**Website / Account #**

**User Name / Email**

**Password / Hint**

**Notes**

**Website / Account #**

**User Name / Email**

**Password / Hint**

**Notes**

**Website / Account #**

**User Name / Email**

**Password / Hint**

**Notes**

**Website / Account #**

**User Name / Email**

**Password / Hint**

**Notes**

**Website / Account #**

**User Name / Email**

**Password / Hint**

**Notes**

**Website / Account #**

**User Name / Email**

**Password / Hint**

**Notes**

**Website / Account #**

**User Name / Email**

**Password / Hint**

**Notes**

**Website / Account #**

**User Name / Email**

**Password / Hint**

**Notes**

**Website / Account #**

---

**User Name / Email**

---

**Password / Hint**

---

**Notes**

---

**Website / Account #**

---

**User Name / Email**

---

**Password / Hint**

---

**Notes**

---

**Website / Account #**

---

**User Name / Email**

---

**Password / Hint**

---

**Notes**

---

**Website / Account #**

**User Name / Email**

**Password / Hint**

**Notes**

**Website / Account #**

**User Name / Email**

**Password / Hint**

**Notes**

**Website / Account #**

**User Name / Email**

**Password / Hint**

**Notes**

**Website / Account #**

**User Name / Email**

**Password / Hint**

**Notes**

**Website / Account #**

**User Name / Email**

**Password / Hint**

**Notes**

**Website / Account #**

**User Name / Email**

**Password / Hint**

**Notes**

**Website / Account #**

**User Name / Email**

**Password / Hint**

**Notes**

**Website / Account #**

**User Name / Email**

**Password / Hint**

**Notes**

**Website / Account #**

**User Name / Email**

**Password / Hint**

**Notes**

**Website / Account #**

**User Name / Email**

**Password / Hint**

**Notes**

**Website / Account #**

**User Name / Email**

**Password / Hint**

**Notes**

**Website / Account #**

**User Name / Email**

**Password / Hint**

**Notes**

**Website / Account #**

**User Name / Email**

**Password / Hint**

**Notes**

**Website / Account #**

**User Name / Email**

**Password / Hint**

**Notes**

**Website / Account #**

**User Name / Email**

**Password / Hint**

**Notes**

**Website / Account #**

**User Name / Email**

**Password / Hint**

**Notes**

**Website / Account #**

**User Name / Email**

**Password / Hint**

**Notes**

**Website / Account #**

**User Name / Email**

**Password / Hint**

**Notes**

**Website / Account #**

**User Name / Email**

**Password / Hint**

**Notes**

**Website / Account #**

**User Name / Email**

**Password / Hint**

**Notes**

**Website / Account #**

**User Name / Email**

**Password / Hint**

**Notes**

**Website / Account #**

**User Name / Email**

**Password / Hint**

**Notes**

G-H

**Website / Account #**

**User Name / Email**

**Password / Hint**

**Notes**

**Website / Account #**

**User Name / Email**

**Password / Hint**

**Notes**

**Website / Account #**

**User Name / Email**

**Password / Hint**

**Notes**

**Website / Account #**

**User Name / Email**

**Password / Hint**

**Notes**

**Website / Account #**

**User Name / Email**

**Password / Hint**

**Notes**

**Website / Account #**

**User Name / Email**

**Password / Hint**

**Notes**

**Website / Account #**

**User Name / Email**

**Password / Hint**

**Notes**

**Website / Account #**

**User Name / Email**

**Password / Hint**

**Notes**

**Website / Account #**

**User Name / Email**

**Password / Hint**

**Notes**

**Website / Account #**

**User Name / Email**

**Password / Hint**

**Notes**

**Website / Account #**

**User Name / Email**

**Password / Hint**

**Notes**

**Website / Account #**

**User Name / Email**

**Password / Hint**

**Notes**

**Website / Account #**

**User Name / Email**

**Password / Hint**

**Notes**

**Website / Account #**

**User Name / Email**

**Password / Hint**

**Notes**

**Website / Account #**

**User Name / Email**

**Password / Hint**

**Notes**

**Website / Account #**

**User Name / Email**

**Password / Hint**

**Notes**

**Website / Account #**

**User Name / Email**

**Password / Hint**

**Notes**

**Website / Account #**

**User Name / Email**

**Password / Hint**

**Notes**

---

**Website / Account #**

**User Name / Email**

**Password / Hint**

**Notes**

---

**Website / Account #**

**User Name / Email**

**Password / Hint**

**Notes**

**Website / Account #**

**User Name / Email**

**Password / Hint**

**Notes**

**Website / Account #**

**User Name / Email**

**Password / Hint**

**Notes**

**Website / Account #**

**User Name / Email**

**Password / Hint**

**Notes**

**Website / Account #**

**User Name / Email**

**Password / Hint**

**Notes**

I-J

**Website / Account #**

**User Name / Email**

**Password / Hint**

**Notes**

**Website / Account #**

**User Name / Email**

**Password / Hint**

**Notes**

**Website / Account #**

**User Name / Email**

**Password / Hint**

**Notes**

**Website / Account #**

**User Name / Email**

**Password / Hint**

**Notes**

**Website / Account #**

**User Name / Email**

**Password / Hint**

**Notes**

**Website / Account #**

**User Name / Email**

**Password / Hint**

**Notes**

**Website / Account #**

**User Name / Email**

**Password / Hint**

**Notes**

**Website / Account #**

**User Name / Email**

**Password / Hint**

**Notes**

**Website / Account #**

**User Name / Email**

**Password / Hint**

**Notes**

**Website / Account #**

**User Name / Email**

**Password / Hint**

**Notes**

**Website / Account #**

**User Name / Email**

**Password / Hint**

**Notes**

**Website / Account #**

**User Name / Email**

**Password / Hint**

**Notes**

**Website / Account #**

**User Name / Email**

**Password / Hint**

**Notes**

**Website / Account #**

**User Name / Email**

**Password / Hint**

**Notes**

**Website / Account #**

**User Name / Email**

**Password / Hint**

**Notes**

**Website / Account #**

**User Name / Email**

**Password / Hint**

**Notes**

**Website / Account #**

**User Name / Email**

**Password / Hint**

**Notes**

**Website / Account #**

**User Name / Email**

**Password / Hint**

**Notes**

**Website / Account #**

**User Name / Email**

**Password / Hint**

**Notes**

**Website / Account #**

**User Name / Email**

**Password / Hint**

**Notes**

**Website / Account #**

**User Name / Email**

**Password / Hint**

**Notes**

**Website / Account #**

**User Name / Email**

**Password / Hint**

**Notes**

**Website / Account #**

**User Name / Email**

**Password / Hint**

**Notes**

**Website / Account #**

**User Name / Email**

**Password / Hint**

**Notes**

**Website / Account #**

K-L

**User Name / Email**

**Password / Hint**

**Notes**

**Website / Account #**

**User Name / Email**

**Password / Hint**

**Notes**

**Website / Account #**

**User Name / Email**

**Password / Hint**

**Notes**

**Website / Account #**

**User Name / Email**

**Password / Hint**

**Notes**

**Website / Account #**

**User Name / Email**

**Password / Hint**

**Notes**

**Website / Account #**

**User Name / Email**

**Password / Hint**

**Notes**

**Website / Account #**

**User Name / Email**

**Password / Hint**

**Notes**

**Website / Account #**

**User Name / Email**

**Password / Hint**

**Notes**

**Website / Account #**

**User Name / Email**

**Password / Hint**

**Notes**

**Website / Account #**

**User Name / Email**

**Password / Hint**

**Notes**

**Website / Account #**

**User Name / Email**

**Password / Hint**

**Notes**

**Website / Account #**

**User Name / Email**

**Password / Hint**

**Notes**

**Website / Account #**

**User Name / Email**

**Password / Hint**

**Notes**

**Website / Account #**

**User Name / Email**

**Password / Hint**

**Notes**

**Website / Account #**

**User Name / Email**

**Password / Hint**

**Notes**

**Website / Account #**

**User Name / Email**

**Password / Hint**

**Notes**

**Website / Account #**

**User Name / Email**

**Password / Hint**

**Notes**

**Website / Account #**

**User Name / Email**

**Password / Hint**

**Notes**

**Website / Account #**

**User Name / Email**

**Password / Hint**

**Notes**

**Website / Account #**

**User Name / Email**

**Password / Hint**

**Notes**

**Website / Account #**

**User Name / Email**

**Password / Hint**

**Notes**

**Website / Account #**

**User Name / Email**

**Password / Hint**

**Notes**

**Website / Account #**

**User Name / Email**

**Password / Hint**

**Notes**

**Website / Account #**

**User Name / Email**

**Password / Hint**

**Notes**

**Website / Account #**

**User Name / Email**

M-N

**Password / Hint**

**Notes**

**Website / Account #**

**User Name / Email**

**Password / Hint**

**Notes**

**Website / Account #**

**User Name / Email**

**Password / Hint**

**Notes**

**Website / Account #**

**User Name / Email**

**Password / Hint**

**Notes**

**Website / Account #**

**User Name / Email**

**Password / Hint**

**Notes**

**Website / Account #**

**User Name / Email**

**Password / Hint**

**Notes**

**Website / Account #**

**User Name / Email**

**Password / Hint**

**Notes**

**Website / Account #**

**User Name / Email**

**Password / Hint**

**Notes**

**Website / Account #**

**User Name / Email**

**Password / Hint**

**Notes**

**Website / Account #**

**User Name / Email**

**Password / Hint**

**Notes**

**Website / Account #**

**User Name / Email**

**Password / Hint**

**Notes**

**Website / Account #**

**User Name / Email**

**Password / Hint**

**Notes**

**Website / Account #**

**User Name / Email**

**Password / Hint**

**Notes**

**Website / Account #**

**User Name / Email**

**Password / Hint**

**Notes**

**Website / Account #**

**User Name / Email**

**Password / Hint**

**Notes**

**Website / Account #**

**User Name / Email**

**Password / Hint**

**Notes**

**Website / Account #**

**User Name / Email**

**Password / Hint**

**Notes**

**Website / Account #**

**User Name / Email**

**Password / Hint**

**Notes**

**Website / Account #**

**User Name / Email**

**Password / Hint**

**Notes**

**Website / Account #**

**User Name / Email**

**Password / Hint**

**Notes**

**Website / Account #**

**User Name / Email**

**Password / Hint**

**Notes**

**Website / Account #**

**User Name / Email**

**Password / Hint**

**Notes**

**Website / Account #**

**User Name / Email**

**Password / Hint**

**Notes**

**Website / Account #**

**User Name / Email**

**Password / Hint**

**Notes**

---

**Website / Account #**

**User Name / Email**

**Password / Hint**

O-P

**Notes**

---

**Website / Account #**

**User Name / Email**

**Password / Hint**

**Notes**

**Website / Account #**

**User Name / Email**

**Password / Hint**

**Notes**

**Website / Account #**

**User Name / Email**

**Password / Hint**

**Notes**

**Website / Account #**

**User Name / Email**

**Password / Hint**

**Notes**

**Website / Account #**

**User Name / Email**

**Password / Hint**

**Notes**

**Website / Account #**

**User Name / Email**

**Password / Hint**

**Notes**

**Website / Account #**

**User Name / Email**

**Password / Hint**

**Notes**

**Website / Account #**

**User Name / Email**

**Password / Hint**

**Notes**

**Website / Account #**

**User Name / Email**

**Password / Hint**

**Notes**

**Website / Account #**

**User Name / Email**

**Password / Hint**

**Notes**

**Website / Account #**

**User Name / Email**

**Password / Hint**

**Notes**

**Website / Account #**

**User Name / Email**

**Password / Hint**

**Notes**

**Website / Account #**

**User Name / Email**

**Password / Hint**

**Notes**

**Website / Account #**

**User Name / Email**

**Password / Hint**

**Notes**

**Website / Account #**

**User Name / Email**

**Password / Hint**

**Notes**

**Website / Account #**

**User Name / Email**

**Password / Hint**

**Notes**

**Website / Account #**

**User Name / Email**

**Password / Hint**

**Notes**

**Website / Account #**

**User Name / Email**

**Password / Hint**

**Notes**

**Website / Account #**

**User Name / Email**

**Password / Hint**

**Notes**

**Website / Account #**

**User Name / Email**

**Password / Hint**

**Notes**

**Website / Account #**

**User Name / Email**

**Password / Hint**

**Notes**

**Website / Account #**

**User Name / Email**

**Password / Hint**

**Notes**

**Website / Account #**

**User Name / Email**

**Password / Hint**

**Notes**

**Website / Account #**

**User Name / Email**

**Password / Hint**

**Notes**

Q-R

**Website / Account #**

**User Name / Email**

**Password / Hint**

**Notes**

**Website / Account #**

**User Name / Email**

**Password / Hint**

**Notes**

**Website / Account #**

**User Name / Email**

**Password / Hint**

**Notes**

**Website / Account #**

**User Name / Email**

**Password / Hint**

**Notes**

**Website / Account #**

**User Name / Email**

**Password / Hint**

**Notes**

**Website / Account #**

**User Name / Email**

**Password / Hint**

**Notes**

**Website / Account #**

**User Name / Email**

**Password / Hint**

**Notes**

**Website / Account #**

**User Name / Email**

**Password / Hint**

**Notes**

**Website / Account #**

**User Name / Email**

**Password / Hint**

**Notes**

**Website / Account #**

**User Name / Email**

**Password / Hint**

**Notes**

**Website / Account #**

**User Name / Email**

**Password / Hint**

**Notes**

**Website / Account #**

**User Name / Email**

**Password / Hint**

**Notes**

**Website / Account #**

**User Name / Email**

**Password / Hint**

**Notes**

**Website / Account #**

**User Name / Email**

**Password / Hint**

**Notes**

**Website / Account #**

**User Name / Email**

**Password / Hint**

**Notes**

**Website / Account #**

**User Name / Email**

**Password / Hint**

**Notes**

**Website / Account #**

**User Name / Email**

**Password / Hint**

**Notes**

**Website / Account #**

**User Name / Email**

**Password / Hint**

**Notes**

**Website / Account #**

**User Name / Email**

**Password / Hint**

**Notes**

**Website / Account #**

**User Name / Email**

**Password / Hint**

**Notes**

**Website / Account #**

**User Name / Email**

**Password / Hint**

**Notes**

**Website / Account #**

**User Name / Email**

**Password / Hint**

**Notes**

**Website / Account #**

**User Name / Email**

**Password / Hint**

**Notes**

**Website / Account #**

**User Name / Email**

**Password / Hint**

**Notes**

**Website / Account #**

S-T

**User Name / Email**

**Password / Hint**

**Notes**

**Website / Account #**

**User Name / Email**

**Password / Hint**

**Notes**

**Website / Account #**

**User Name / Email**

**Password / Hint**

**Notes**

**Website / Account #**

**User Name / Email**

**Password / Hint**

**Notes**

**Website / Account #**

**User Name / Email**

**Password / Hint**

**Notes**

**Website / Account #**

**User Name / Email**

**Password / Hint**

**Notes**

**Website / Account #**

**User Name / Email**

**Password / Hint**

**Notes**

**Website / Account #**

**User Name / Email**

**Password / Hint**

**Notes**

**Website / Account #**

**User Name / Email**

**Password / Hint**

**Notes**

**Website / Account #**

**User Name / Email**

**Password / Hint**

**Notes**

**Website / Account #**

**User Name / Email**

**Password / Hint**

**Notes**

**Website / Account #**

**User Name / Email**

**Password / Hint**

**Notes**

**Website / Account #**

**User Name / Email**

**Password / Hint**

**Notes**

**Website / Account #**

**User Name / Email**

**Password / Hint**

**Notes**

**Website / Account #**

**User Name / Email**

**Password / Hint**

**Notes**

**Website / Account #**

**User Name / Email**

**Password / Hint**

**Notes**

**Website / Account #**

**User Name / Email**

**Password / Hint**

**Notes**

**Website / Account #**

**User Name / Email**

**Password / Hint**

**Notes**

**Website / Account #**

**User Name / Email**

**Password / Hint**

**Notes**

**Website / Account #**

**User Name / Email**

**Password / Hint**

**Notes**

**Website / Account #**

**User Name / Email**

**Password / Hint**

**Notes**

**Website / Account #**

**User Name / Email**

**Password / Hint**

**Notes**

**Website / Account #**

**User Name / Email**

**Password / Hint**

**Notes**

**Website / Account #**

**User Name / Email**

**Password / Hint**

**Notes**

**Website / Account #**

**User Name / Email**

U-V

**Password / Hint**

**Notes**

**Website / Account #**

**User Name / Email**

**Password / Hint**

**Notes**

**Website / Account #**

**User Name / Email**

**Password / Hint**

**Notes**

**Website / Account #**

**User Name / Email**

**Password / Hint**

**Notes**

**Website / Account #**

**User Name / Email**

**Password / Hint**

**Notes**

**Website / Account #**

**User Name / Email**

**Password / Hint**

**Notes**

**Website / Account #**

**User Name / Email**

**Password / Hint**

**Notes**

**Website / Account #**

**User Name / Email**

**Password / Hint**

**Notes**

**Website / Account #**

**User Name / Email**

**Password / Hint**

**Notes**

**Website / Account #**

**User Name / Email**

**Password / Hint**

**Notes**

**Website / Account #**

**User Name / Email**

**Password / Hint**

**Notes**

**Website / Account #**

**User Name / Email**

**Password / Hint**

**Notes**

**Website / Account #**

**User Name / Email**

**Password / Hint**

**Notes**

**Website / Account #**

**User Name / Email**

**Password / Hint**

**Notes**

**Website / Account #**

**User Name / Email**

**Password / Hint**

**Notes**

**Website / Account #**

**User Name / Email**

**Password / Hint**

**Notes**

**Website / Account #**

**User Name / Email**

**Password / Hint**

**Notes**

**Website / Account #**

**User Name / Email**

**Password / Hint**

**Notes**

**Website / Account #**

**User Name / Email**

**Password / Hint**

**Notes**

**Website / Account #**

**User Name / Email**

**Password / Hint**

**Notes**

**Website / Account #**

**User Name / Email**

**Password / Hint**

**Notes**

**Website / Account #**

**User Name / Email**

**Password / Hint**

**Notes**

**Website / Account #**

**User Name / Email**

**Password / Hint**

**Notes**

**Website / Account #**

**User Name / Email**

**Password / Hint**

**Notes**

**Website / Account #**

**User Name / Email**

**Password / Hint**

W-X

**Notes**

**Website / Account #**

**User Name / Email**

**Password / Hint**

**Notes**

**Website / Account #**

**User Name / Email**

**Password / Hint**

**Notes**

**Website / Account #**

**User Name / Email**

**Password / Hint**

**Notes**

**Website / Account #**

**User Name / Email**

**Password / Hint**

**Notes**

**Website / Account #**

**User Name / Email**

**Password / Hint**

**Notes**

**Website / Account #**

**User Name / Email**

**Password / Hint**

**Notes**

**Website / Account #**

---

**User Name / Email**

---

**Password / Hint**

---

**Notes**

---

**Website / Account #**

---

**User Name / Email**

---

**Password / Hint**

---

**Notes**

---

**Website / Account #**

---

**User Name / Email**

---

**Password / Hint**

---

**Notes**

---

**Website / Account #**

**User Name / Email**

**Password / Hint**

**Notes**

**Website / Account #**

**User Name / Email**

**Password / Hint**

**Notes**

**Website / Account #**

**User Name / Email**

**Password / Hint**

**Notes**

**Website / Account #**

**User Name / Email**

**Password / Hint**

**Notes**

**Website / Account #**

**User Name / Email**

**Password / Hint**

**Notes**

**Website / Account #**

**User Name / Email**

**Password / Hint**

**Notes**

**Website / Account #**

**User Name / Email**

**Password / Hint**

**Notes**

**Website / Account #**

**User Name / Email**

**Password / Hint**

**Notes**

**Website / Account #**

**User Name / Email**

**Password / Hint**

**Notes**

**Website / Account #**

**User Name / Email**

**Password / Hint**

**Notes**

**Website / Account #**

**User Name / Email**

**Password / Hint**

**Notes**

**Website / Account #**

**User Name / Email**

**Password / Hint**

**Notes**

**Website / Account #**

**User Name / Email**

**Password / Hint**

**Notes**

**Website / Account #**

**User Name / Email**

**Password / Hint**

**Notes**

**Website / Account #**

**User Name / Email**

**Password / Hint**

**Notes**

Y-Z

**Website / Account #**

**User Name / Email**

**Password / Hint**

**Notes**

**Website / Account #**

**User Name / Email**

**Password / Hint**

**Notes**

**Website / Account #**

**User Name / Email**

**Password / Hint**

**Notes**

**Website / Account #**

**User Name / Email**

**Password / Hint**

**Notes**

**Website / Account #**

**User Name / Email**

**Password / Hint**

**Notes**

**Website / Account #**

**User Name / Email**

**Password / Hint**

**Notes**

**Website / Account #**

**User Name / Email**

**Password / Hint**

**Notes**

**Website / Account #**

**User Name / Email**

**Password / Hint**

**Notes**

**Website / Account #**

**User Name / Email**

**Password / Hint**

**Notes**

**Website / Account #**

**User Name / Email**

**Password / Hint**

**Notes**

**Website / Account #**

**User Name / Email**

**Password / Hint**

**Notes**

**Website / Account #**

**User Name / Email**

**Password / Hint**

**Notes**

**Website / Account #**

---

**User Name / Email**

---

**Password / Hint**

---

**Notes**

---

**Website / Account #**

---

**User Name / Email**

---

**Password / Hint**

---

**Notes**

---

**Website / Account #**

---

**User Name / Email**

---

**Password / Hint**

---

**Notes**

---

**Website / Account #**

**User Name / Email**

**Password / Hint**

**Notes**

**Website / Account #**

**User Name / Email**

**Password / Hint**

**Notes**

**Website / Account #**

**User Name / Email**

**Password / Hint**

**Notes**